TABLE OF CONTENTS

MW00929109

Arkansas Traveler

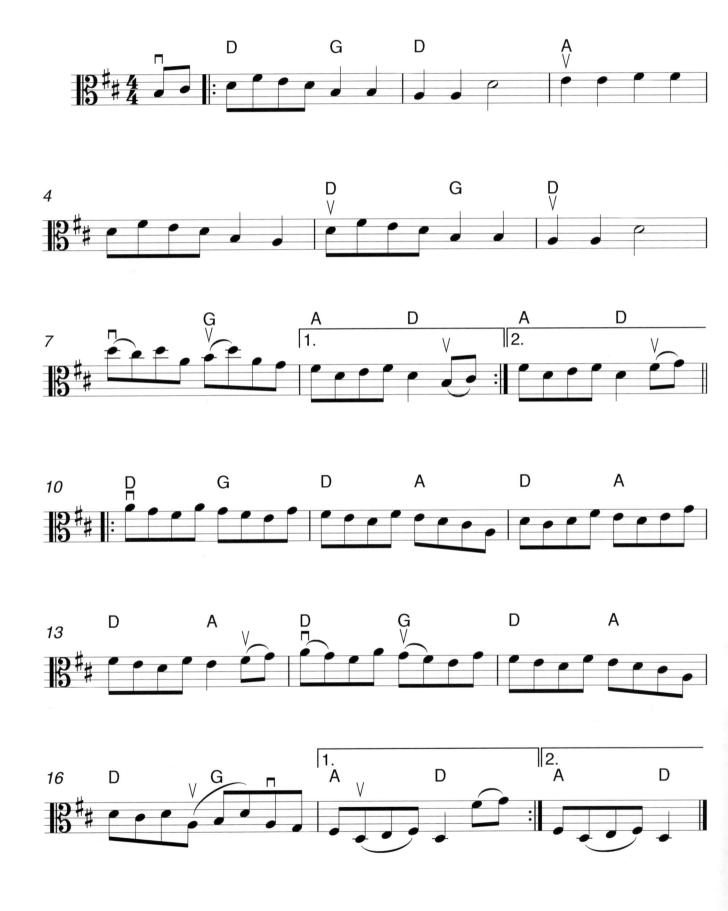

Bill Cheatum

Blackberry Blossom

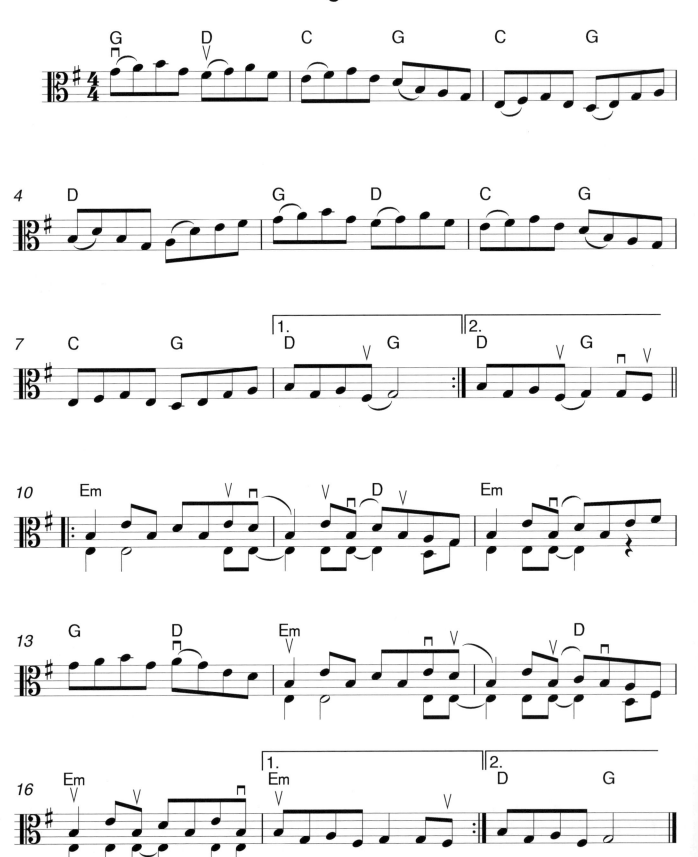

Black Eyed Suzie

Boil Them Cabbage Down

Buffalo Gals

Cluck Old Hen

Cluckin' Hen

Devil's Dream

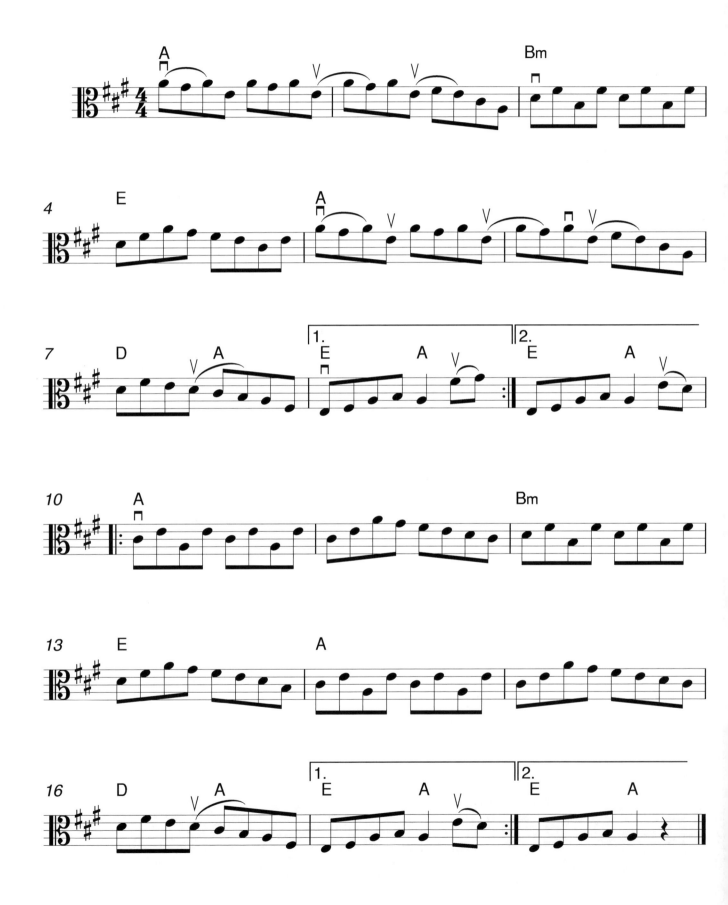

Ebenezer

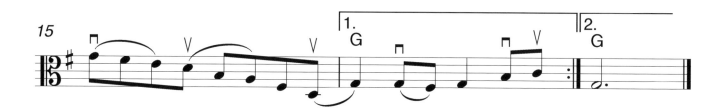

Fiddler's Dream

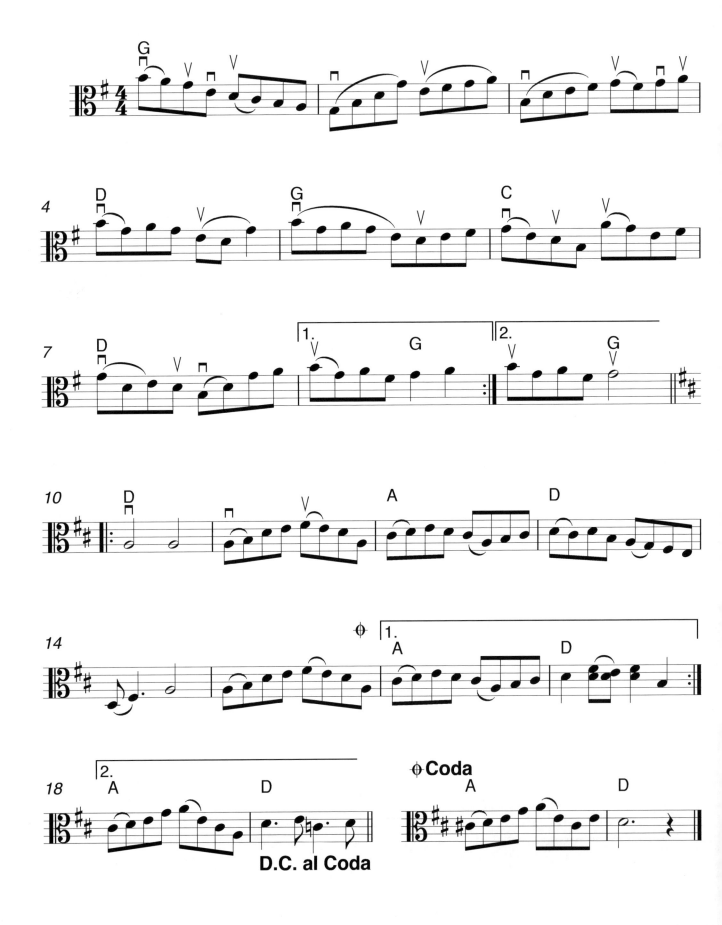

Fiddling Around

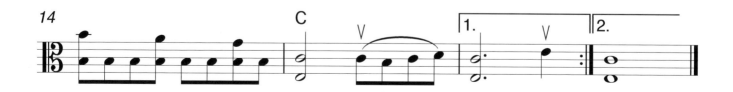

Fire on the Mountain

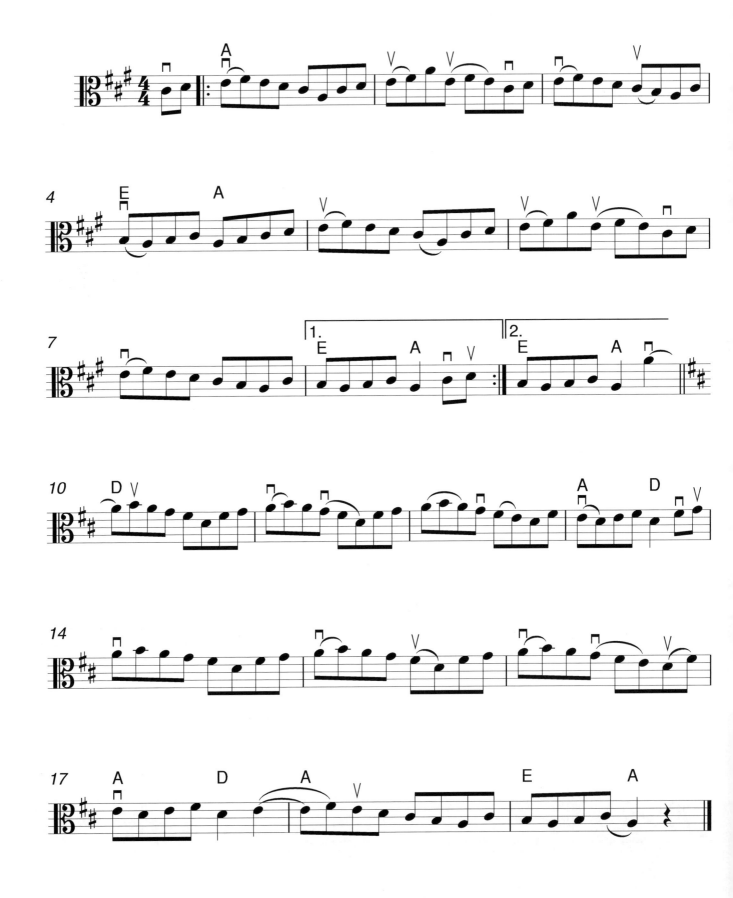

Girl I Left Behind Me

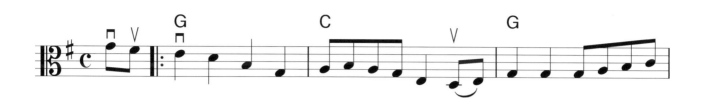

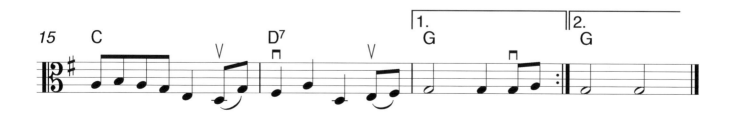

Goodbye Liza Jane

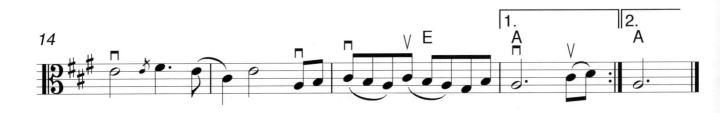

Great Big Taters in Sandyland

Hickman County

Jenny Lind Polka

Liberty

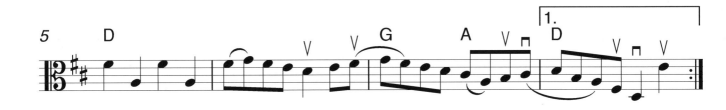

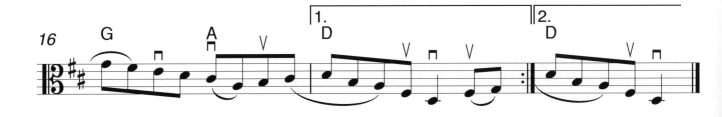

Off to California

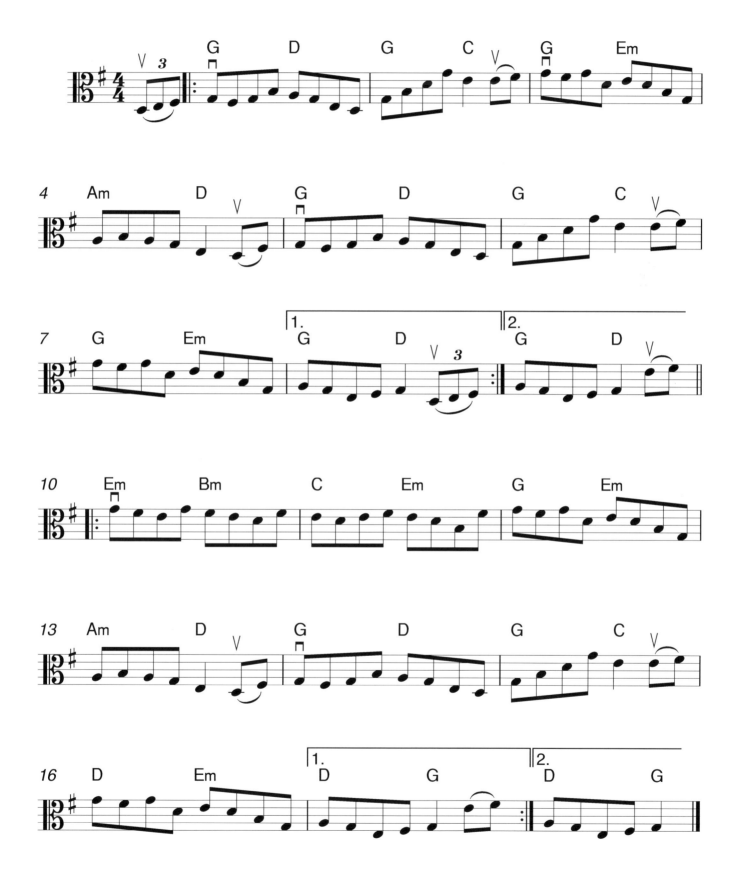

Old Joe Clark

one More River to Cross

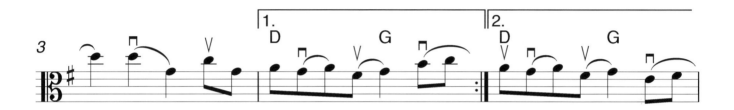

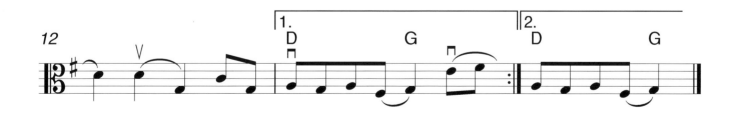

Pick a Bale of Cotton

Pig Ankle Rag

Redwing

Rock The Cradle Joe

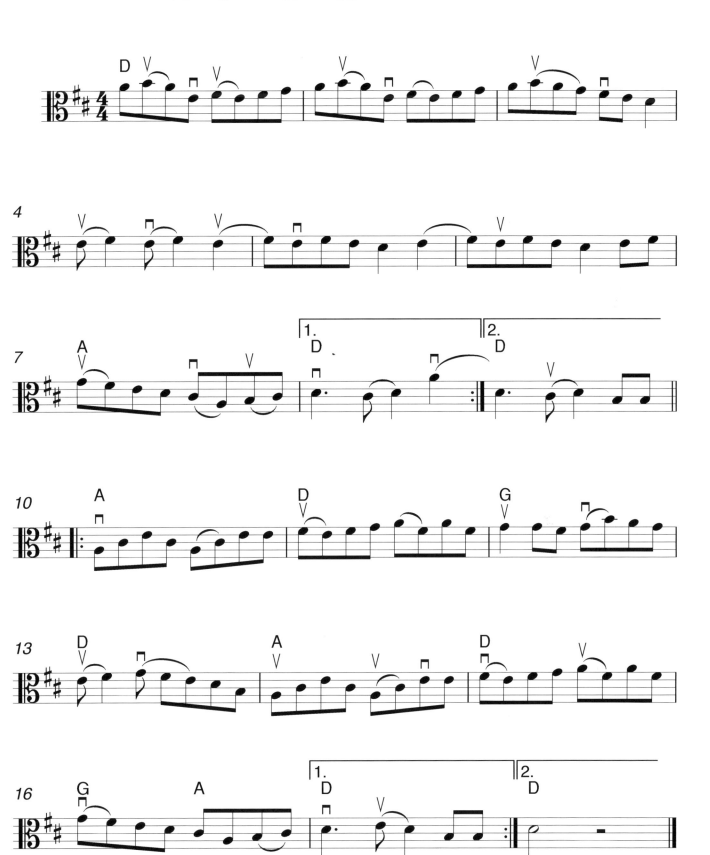

Sally Gooden

Shortnin' Bread

shoot the Turkey Buzzard

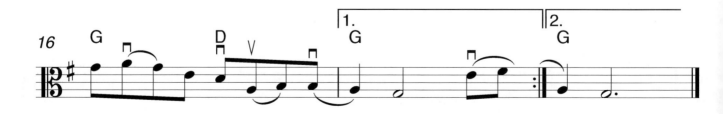

soldier's Dream

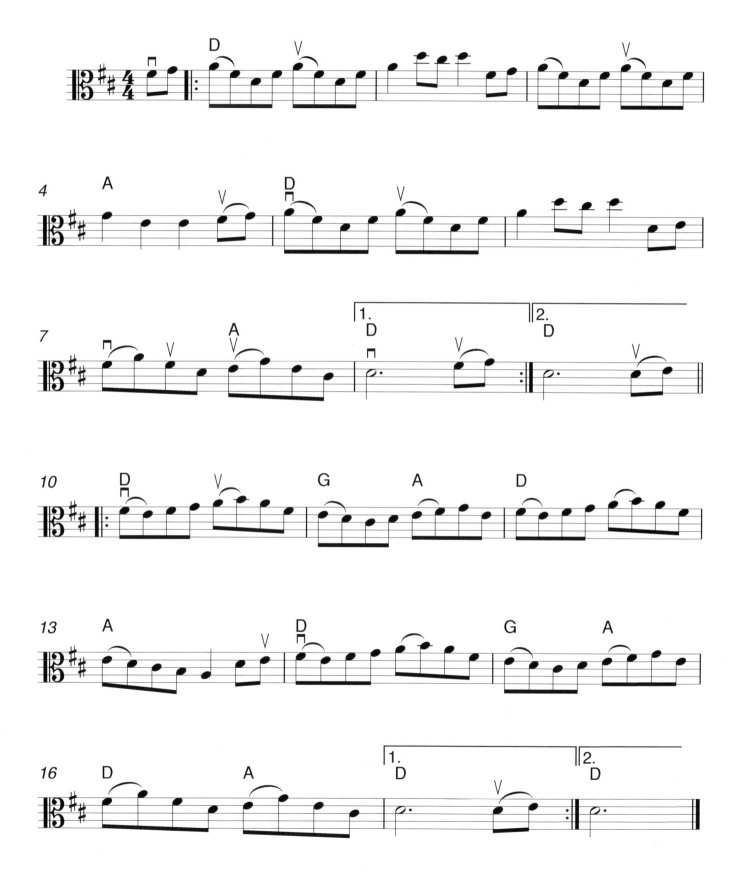

Stone's Rag

Sweet Bunch of Daisies

Three-In-One Two Step

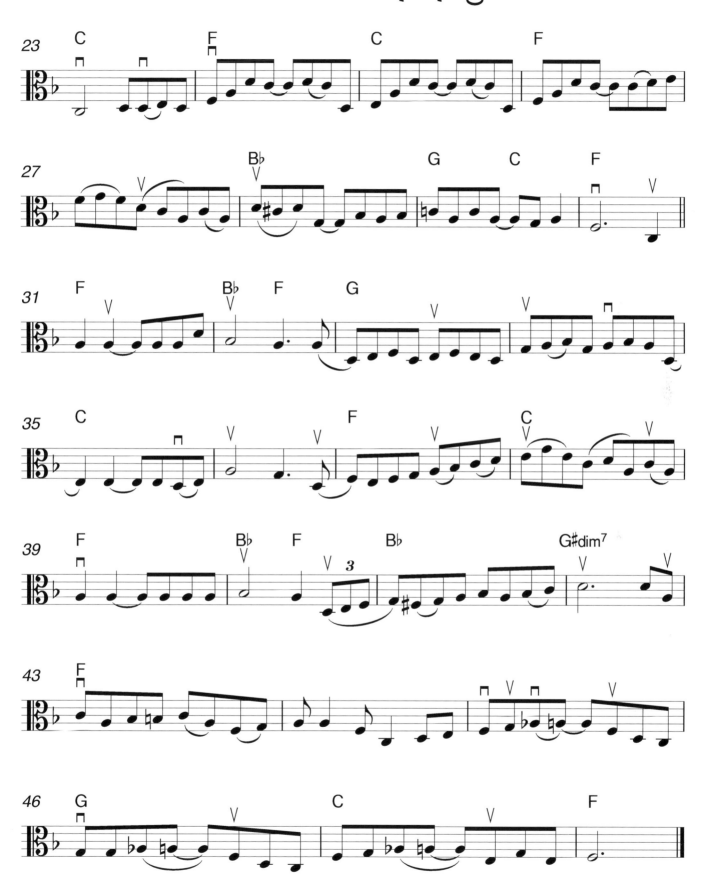

Tom and Jerry

Too Young to Marry

Turkey in the straw

Made in the USA
Middletown, DE
01 December 2019